BAD PEOPLE

A PLAY BY KATI SCHWARTZ

Copyright © 2023 Bad People Audio LLC

www.KatiSchwartz.com

ISBN: 979-8-9875127-1-5

All rights reserved. No part of this publication may be reproduced, distributed, performed, or transmitted in any form or by any means without the prior written permission of the publisher, except in the case of brief quotations embodied in critical reviews and certain other uses permitted by copyright law.

For inquiries, contact Kati Schwartz,
www.KatiSchwartz.com.

Bad People Audio LLC Publishers

***Bad People* is dedicated**

to those brave enough to tell,

and those brave enough to say, "Me too."

About the Author

Kati Schwartz's play **The Coward** premiered Off Broadway at The Duke Theatre as part of the New York New Works Festival 2017, which she won. Her play **She Got Off The Couch** premiered at the Hollywood Fringe Festival in 2016 where it received the Producers Encore Award and was extended twice. Other plays, including **The Whale Play** and **Caring for The Dead,** featuring original music by For You The Moon, have been produced all over the country. Her work has twice been a semifinalist for the Eugene O'Neill National Playwrights Conference.

Contents

Characters in Order of Appearance   v

Disclaimer   vi

Prologue   1

Part I - Agony

    The 27 Club   6

    Object Permanence   17

Part II - The Part That Started Around The Time I Tried To Face The Horizon, Stretch My Arms Out, And Say , "I Accept And Love Myself Exactly As I Am." And I Then Thought, "That's Not Possible."

    The Triggered   36

    The Day the Music Died   43

Part III — There Are Some Things That I'm Finally Ready To Say Like They Are And Not Make Them Seem Better Or Different Than They Were.

    The Journal   57

    Heealthy Relationships   67

    Middle Earth   77

CHARACTERS IN ORDER OF APPEARANCE

Narrator (Me Now)
Me (Back Then)
Ellen
Sharon
Mormon
Yurt Woman
Chad
Fedex Worker
Little Monster
Alex
Michael
Logan
Dr. Kerr
Coffee Meets Bagel Girl
Marcy
Random Male Friend
Diane
Voices 1-22
Old Friend
Aunt's Facebook Status
Barista 1 and 2

DISCLAIMER

Bad people is a work of creative nonfiction and is not an indictment of any real life person or group of people.

PROLOGUE

[Narrator enters the stage.]

NARRATOR Hi everyone! Wow, hi .... Thank you so much for "tuning in." I thi,nk that's what you say for a podcast, right? This is my first time doing this, so I really don't know what's going on. But I'm here! I'm doing it!

Before we really get started, I just wanted to share a fun little tidbit about me. So, I really love *Lord of The Rings*. Like ... really, really ... really like *Lord of the Rings*. Or anything by Tolkien, really. If you've read anything that takes place in Middle Earth, we can be friends.

So, I'd been really scared to tell this story, and then just recently I read *Barely Functional Adult* by Meichi Ng, which is an amazing graphic memoir. And she has this really great quote at the start of the book. She says "Don't forget. We write our own stories. And we can write whatever the hell we want."

This is my story. I wrote it for me. I wrote whatever the hell I wanted. It's my truth, the way I lived it.

This story is a lot for me. Maybe not for any other people, but for me ... it's always so hard for me to tell. I get so nervous! And I'm a nervous babbler, which is not great when your show has time parameters like this one! So ... okay, what do I have to tell you before we start? Well, okay! First! Like I said, my name is ... well actually it doesn't matter what my name is right now. Right now, I'm the Narrator. I am the writer of this show and the liver of this story. That sounds like I'm an organ. Like a liver liver, ha. But no, I'm ....

Let's see ... a trigger warning? Maybe? I used to make fun

of those, and then I went and saw this play on Broadway that super triggered me and ... wow. That wasn't fun. And they didn't warn me beforehand or anything .... So ... yeah. Here's your warning. Okay ... and please, feel free to leave if any of this is too much. So: Trigger warning. This is a story of ... Grooming. Indoctrination. A ... powerful man ... is that a trigger? Powerful man trigger? Man who abuses his power. What about just "abusive man?" Just "abuse?" Is that better?

Because that's kind of what this show is about. My experience with an abusive man who indoctrinated me into his weird, cultish world. My Me Too Movement story, you could say. But said abusive man isn't even introduced right away ... his character doesn't come into the story for a while. And I guess I sort of begin a journey towards "self love" by the end. Or something. So maybe that's what it's about?

I'm babbling. The good news is that after you leave tonight you get to form your own opinions on everything I say.

Oh another trigger before we start: suicidal ideation. That one only lasts a moment. But still, it's in the first part .... Let's just get started okay? I'll check in and say hey from time to time. But for now....

Okay....

KATI SCHWARTZ

BAD PEOPLE

KATI SCHWARTZ

PART I - Agony

THE 27 CLUB

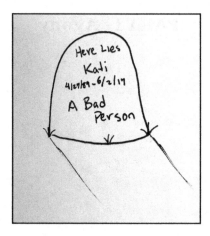

NARRATOR: Sometimes it feels like every great musician I've ever loved died super young. Some of my absolute favorites. Like … Janis Joplin. Jimi Hendrix. Kurt Cobain. Amy Winehouse. There's nothing I wouldn't give to see any of those people in concert!

What's really weird is that all of those guys died at age 27. That's kind of freaky, right? All of them died in totally different ways, but all at the exact same age. And there are so many more of them. If you Google "The 27 Club," you'll find a massive list of amazingly talented people who died at 27. It's kind of morbidly fascinating. And that's what it's called: The 27 Club.

Funnily enough … on May 28th, 2016, shortly after my own 27th birthday, my world as I knew it ended. I was leaving an afternoon appointment in Glendale, California, when I received a text from my dear friend Sharon, telling me I'd been "caught." I'd told a lie about a friend, and I'd been found out. This text was my official ousting notice from my beloved group of friends, all of whom I'd come to consider my "everything."

The lie I told was said to Sharon.

ME: Ellen told me that I should disappear.

NARRATOR That was me.

NARRATOR [CONT'D] This, me talking right now, is *now me*. This ...

ME: (Same voice, sounding a little naive.) Ellen told me that I should disappear.

NARRATOR ... is *back then* me. (Sounding a little less naive.) **Now me**.

ME: *Back then* me.

NARRATOR Got it? So, I said that Ellen told me I should disappear.

Ellen had never told me that I should disappear. When Ellen found out what I'd said she responded with:

ELLEN: I would NEVER tell you to disappear.

NARRATOR This comeback was followed by a 'sad face' emoji. Then she said:

ELLEN: I guess all the times I was being nice to you, you really just thought I was being mean.

NARRATOR: That was the last time I ever heard from her. Or any of them.

To say these people were my friends is an understatement. I'd moved to LA a year and a half earlier after years of floundering in New York. Once I met them, I felt like I'd landed. It was like when Google Maps says "you've arrived" after a twelve hour car trip. They were all multi-hyphenate, incredible self motivated artists. They made me feel like I didn't have to label myself as "actor" or "writer." I could just live in art every day. And they took me in as if they'd been waiting for me. I lived in a spare room in the house where several of them lived. I lived with them not in a roommate way. In a family way. They introduced me to my first real girlfriend. They were my people. They were my family, my fellow silly artists, and people I'd laugh myself to sleep with on the living room floor. I'd wake up everyday wondering how I was lucky enough to have been chosen by them.

Although the lie I told about my friend was fairly innocuous and not mean-spirited, it hit all her areas of insecurity, and thus was probably the most hurtful thing I could have done to her. That, combined with the fact that Chad, the informal "leader" of this family, had little tolerance for "bad behavior," as he called it, resulted in me being exiled. I spent hours and days and months wondering why on earth I couldn't have just held it together and NOT done that.

The thing is, I have a theory that everyone has their own stupid little monster that comes forward when they're in pain. It can be the lying and exaggeration monster, or the lashing out monster, or passive aggressive monster, or everyone-reminds-me-of-my-ex- girlfriend monster. The day I sent that text, my terrified little monster woke up, reared its head, and showed me that I, just like everyone else when they're in pain, have the ability to act out of character and hurt the people I most love.

After reading Sharon's text, I felt the world around me dissolve. I saw two words materialize in front of my face:

BAD. PERSON.

Those two words were my new identity; the description others would use when speaking of me. What else could I be called after what I'd done?

So, at this point, you might find yourself thinking, "She didn't do anything that bad." Allow me to paint a clearer picture of how bad I believed myself to be: Before this happened, Sharon, who loves all things dark and disturbing, had told me about The Slender Man.

The setting: Sharon's very nice house in Los Angeles.

SHARON: Have you heard of The Slender Man?

ME: What's that?

SHARON: It's a myth about this weird skinny guy with really long arms and legs who steals children.

ME: Is he real?

SHARON: Maybe. He might be.

ME: Wow.

SHARON: But these two like twelve year old girls thought he was for sure real, and that he was like coming to get them or something. And that if they didn't want him to steal them they had to kill their best friend. So they did.

ME: They killed their best friend!?

SHARON: Well, no. They just stabbed her a lot. But she almost died.

ME: Oh my god.

SHARON: There's a documentary about it.

NARRATOR: We watched it. It was just as disturbing as I expected.

SHARON: Isn't this awesome?

ME: This is freaky.

SHARON: Would you do that to me?

ME: Try to kill you?

SHARON: Yeah.

ME: Of course not.

SHARON: Even if The Slender Man was going to take you?

ME: I'd never do that to you.

NARRATOR: After reading Sharon's text telling me she knew what I'd done, one of my first thoughts was:

ME: I am worse than those twelve year old girls.

NARRATOR: The ones who stabbed their best friend ten times in the back.

ME: I basically stabbed Ellen twenty times in the back.

NARRATOR: I felt, for the first time, that taking my own life might be the only option left, as I now had nothing. Amid my incomprehensible texts and voicemails to Sharon begging to be understood and forgiven, I stumbled towards my car. Before I got there, I was stopped by a young Mormon missionary.

MORMON: Hello! Do you have a moment to talk about the Church of Jesus Christ of Latter Day Saints?"

ME: No. Not really.

MORMON: Can I give you this pamphlet?

ME: Okay.

NARRATOR: I took it.

MORMON: I hope you have a beautiful day!

ME: Thank you. I won't.

MORMON: I'm sorry?

ME: I've just lost everything. So I won't have a beautiful day.

MORMON: Maybe if you let Jesus Christ into your heart you could ....

ME: Jesus could never love someone like me.

MORMON: That's not true. Jesus loves everyone.

ME: I'm a bad person. Satan might love me but not Jesus.

MORMON: I think you might find some clarity if you let me explain the foundations of the Mormon religion. You see ....

ME: Fuck you.

NARRATOR: I got into my car, and drove mindlessly. I didn't know where I was going. I didn't know if I was going to drive off a cliff. I just drove. Ignoring every "Don't Text And Drive" sign, I shouted at Siri to send endless text messages to the friends I'd hurt, asking for another chance. Trying to explain myself, to apologize, or receive some sort of confirmation that I could still be let back in. They didn't respond.

Before I knew it, it was dark, and I was 300 miles up the coast of California right next to Big Sur. I got out of my car and walked out to one of the cliffs looking over the ocean. The stars reflected off the surf, creating the dizzying illusion that I was surrounded by undulating sky. I felt like I was seeing the universe.

I felt the presence of Janis, Amy, Kurt, of all those artists who had reached their 27th year and decided not to go on. I was reminded of the lyrics to my favorite Janis Joplin song:

ME: (Singing.)

One of these mornings be proud and fair, Put on my wings and then I'll try the air Since it looks like everybody in this whole round world, Is down on me. Down on me.

NARRATOR: I remember thinking, "what would the rest of Janet's life have been like?" And, "I wonder what 28-year-old Amy would tell me to do." Their lyrics and music had guided me for most of my life. Would they really tell me there was no point in living?

In that moment, I made the decision not to join the 27 Club. I decided to stay alive.

That night, I stayed in a Yurt on a middle aged woman's tulip farm.

YURT WOMAN: Do me a favor: don't give me a review on AirBnb. No pictures on social media, no thank you notes, no nothing. I'm not supposed to have property here, and if the feds find out I'm running an AirBnb, they'll take away my tulips.

ME: The feds?

YURT WOMAN: Just don't do it kid. Or you'll be sleeping in the park.

NARRATOR: I spared her the rest of my story, and spent my night in her yurt making lists. The first one read:

ME: Things to do:

-Find a therapist.

-Ask around for a basement to live in until friends are willing to take me back.

-Write apology letters.

-Book plane ticket back to New York.

NARRATOR: The second one read:

ME: Reasons to Live:

-Dogs

-Other animals

-Seeing my play on Broadway

-Things might get better (???)

-Lord of the Rings

-Just got a tattoo

-Seeing my published book in a bookstore.

NARRATOR:

Those lists were the first tiny baby steps that began a process of growth, discovery, unbelievable pain, moments of despair, moments of love, and attempts to turn my pain into art.

One of those attempts was the idea to make a bunch of weird art about what came after my 27th year, aka the year I decided to keep living. So here it is: this is my artistic expression of what happened.

OBJECT PERMANENCE

NARRATOR: Before we start talking about Chad, I want to tell you about this baby I saw on the subway. It'll be quick, I promise.

I'd been back in New York for a couple of months since leaving LA, and I was on the 1 train. There was this baby across from me with the biggest eyeballs I'd ever seen. They were frickin' huge. So I'm staring at these giant eyeballs and they're staring back, and then I'm hit with this intoxicating feeling of power. I know I can make the baby laugh! I cover my face with my hands. I take a deep breath and quickly remove my hands, simultaneously contorting my face into a misshapen expression of surprise.

I'm ... realizing this story isn't actually that interesting. All that happened was that the baby laughed and then stared at me with its big eyes waiting for more. So I did it again. And again. And again. And then I got off the train. It was a pretty standard game of peekaboo. But the point I'm trying to make is that I AM that baby.

According to my Wikipedia search, young children love peekaboo because their teeny developing brains are learning to understand object permanence.

Object permanence is the understanding that someone or something exists even when it can't be seen. When a baby's parent leaves a room, until this understanding is developed, the baby has no sense that the person will ever return. They will scream and cry when their parent walks into the kitchen or bathroom, and then freak out with joy when they return. These principals are what make peekaboo so exciting for them. A human face is present, goes away seemingly FOREVER, and then ... surprise!! It's still there!

So, at this time, I was 26. That's way older than most peekaboo participants. But I'd found myself in a never ending game of it. After almost seven years of fruitless auditioning and failed attempts to fit in with literally anyone in New York, I'd had some sort of, like, artistic crisis and moved to southern California. I was so far away from everyone I knew, in a city I'd never even been to before. I was literally all by myself, and isolated in a way I'd never known before. Needless to say, I was in a vulnerable place to say the least. But then, kind of out of nowhere, I quickly developed one of the most intimately close friendships I've ever experienced.

CHAD: You're not just my best friend, you're my sister. And I love you.

NARRATOR: This is Chad. Chad's the guy I told you about at the start. Chad was ... the coolest and most famous person I'd ever met. He was nearing forty - more than a decade older than most of his friends and at least two decades older than the women he wooed and slept with. He wasn't just a famous musician, he was a famous Rock Star.

Okay, so now that he's finally here, I know you're all wondering who this person is. Isn't it so juicy when you find out someone you know knows a famous person!?

I'm not going to tell you who it is. He has a lot of money and could easily fuck up my life.

The first time I met Chad, I'd been hired to be a PA on a music video he was shooting. Our first real encounter lives very clearly in my mind.

NARRATOR: Setting: Chad's on-set dressing room. He's sitting on the floor. I've just run some errands for him.

ME: Here are your Cheerios.

CHAD: Thank you so much.

NARRATOR: I started to leave.

CHAD: Can you stay? I'm having a really hard time and I need a friend.

ME: Do you want me to get ... ?

CHAD: No, I want you.

NARRATOR: I sat on the floor with him.

ME: My name is ....

CHAD: I know who you are.

ME: I didn't think you'd remember.

CHAD: Of course, I do.

ME: That's so nice.

CHAD: I'm going through a breakup.

ME: I'm so sorry. That's awful.

CHAD: Thanks for being here for me.

NARRATOR: We sat like that for several hours. The shoot got super behind schedule because he wanted to keep talking with me. I wasn't used to someone trusting me that quickly.

CHAD: She had the same name as you.

ME: Your ex?

CHAD: Yeah.

ME: Is it weird?

CHAD: No. I like it.

NARRATOR: Sitting there with him, I felt like I'd won some lottery I didn't know I'd entered. He was a star, and he made me feel lucky to be talking to him.

CHAD: It's hard to get close to people when everyone knows who you are.

ME: I didn't know who you were until now.

CHAD: It's a relief.

NARRATOR: We talked for an insanely long time.

ME: I think the more you try to push away your breakup pain, the longer it will stick around. You have to feel it and come out the other side.

CHAD: Wow. That's amazing advice.

ME: Thanks.

CHAD: I'm so glad you're in my life.

NARRATOR: Anyway, after that, Chad and I were inseparable.

NARRATOR: Setting: Living room floor.

ME: Stop saying "chode."

CHAD: It is my god given right to say chode as many times as I want.

ME: The word chode makes me want to vomit.

CHAD: (Whispering.) Chode.

ME: Here's what I need you to do: I need you to go into the back yard and impale yourself with a pitchfork.

CHAD: I have a dare for you.

ME: Don't change the subject.

CHAD: See if you can wash all the dishes without getting your hands wet.

ME: I'm adding chode to the list of words we can't say.

CHAD: And you can't wear gloves either.

ME: I'm still talking about chodes!!

CHAD: You're saying it way more than I am.

ME: It's your fault.

NARRATOR: There we also serious conversations.
   Setting: Under the lemon tree in the back yard.

ME: Have you ever had someone you love die?

CHAD: No, not really. You?

ME: My friend Taylor killed herself.

CHAD: Whoa.

ME: Two years ago.

CHAD: Holy shit dude.

ME: I'm still sad about it.

CHAD: Makes sense. Death is a form of abandonment.

ME: I guess so.

CHAD: It is. Especially suicide.

ME: Do you think about death a lot?

CHAD: It scares me.

ME: Me too.

CHAD: I promise I won't ever do that to you.

ME: Die?

CHAD: Abandon you.

ME: Wow.

NARRATOR: It was exactly what I'd always wanted to hear.

[Beat.]

CHAD: Hey, by the way, could you come into the recording studio with me tomorrow just to hang? I've been feeling sad about my breakup again and it would be really comforting just to have you there.

ME: I'd love nothing more.

CHAD: You're such a good person.

NARRATOR: Before I knew it, we were enmeshed. We felt like one person.

NARRATOR: Setting: Fedex print center. A Fedex worker stands behind a counter. Chad and I are laughing at each other.

FEDEX WORKER: Are you two siblings? You look like it.

CHAD: No we're just best friends. I can't function without her, so we're never too far from each other.

NARRATOR: They also sounded like this:

    Setting: text messages.

ME: Is everything okay? I haven't heard from you for two hours.

CHAD: I was at the dentist.

ME: You didn't invite me?

NARRATOR: One night after returning from a weekend trip, he asked me to accompany him on a drive to the post office. I could tell immediately that something was suddenly very different.

Setting: Chad's car with heated seats and Bose speakers. Chad has the fanciest car.

ME: Can't you just mail your rent from the mailbox on the corner?

CHAD: I like to move around when having difficult conversations. It's like how babies like to be bounced when they're upset. It's comforting.

ME: Are we having a "difficult conversation?"

CHAD: Not necessarily.

ME: Okay ....

CHAD: Can we agree to try seeing each other only once a week?

ME: What?

CHAD: I've been thinking about it for a while but I didn't want to tell you yet.

ME: Okay ... I guess.

NARRATOR: This was prime food for my "don't abandon me" little monster.

CHAD: It'll be healthier that way.

ME: What changed?

CHAD: Why do you think something changed? I'm just Setting Boundaries.

ME: Okay.

CHAD: As long as you can respect my needs we'll be friends for a long time.

NARRATOR: I was so determined to comply. But something felt ominous. My resolve held for maybe 24 hours. After that, I was hit with an overwhelming feeling that can only be described as homesickness. Home isn't always a place, sometimes it's a person. Without my realizing it, this man had become my home. And I was losing him.

    Setting: Chad's doorstep. Midnight.

ME: When will I see you again?

CHAD: Next week. I already said that.

ME: I can't wait that long.

CHAD: Try.

NARRATOR: Chad closed the door. I knocked on the door. Chad opened the door.

CHAD: I need to sleep.

ME: Can I stay for five more minutes?

NARRATOR: I felt myself growing steadily more annoying with each interaction. At this point in my life, I'd had little to no demonstration of healthy boundaries, and felt no ability to control or remedy my behavior. At the time, I was working as a nanny for a two year old girl. I'd watch her scream "MAMA!!!!!!" and bang her fists against the closed door to the room where her mother was trying to work. She'd throw her head back in comical toddler grief and hiccup with sobs. During one of these tantrums, I was struck by the nauseating similarity between her and myself.

Remember the whole thing of someone's here, then they're not? She and I were feeling the same thing.

NARRATOR: One night, I left Chad's house after a hang out session.

Setting: Chad's living room. Again.

ME: Are you going to eat the last piece of your spicy tuna roll?

CHAD: You can have it.

[Silence.]

CHAD: Put on that Janis Joplin song?

ME: Which one?

CHAD: The one where she's obsessed with that guy.

ME: Sorry that I'm -

CHAD: It's not your fault. All girls are crazy. I just thought you were different.

ME: Yeah.

[Pause. Me and Bobby McGee by Janis Joplin plays.]

ME (CONT'D): Have you heard of the 27 Club?

NARRATOR: As I drove my car away from Chad's house, panic rose in my chest. I felt insane. My little monster showed up to talk to me.

   Setting: My car.

ME: I'm going to drive home.

LITTLE MONSTER: You need Chad.

ME: I don't need Chad. I'm an adult.

LITTLE MONSTER: What if he's gone?

ME: Gone?

LITTLE MONSTER: What if you never see him again?

ME: Leave me alone.

LITTLE MONSTER: Like he said. All girls are crazy. You're crazy.

ME: Are all girls actually crazy?

LITTLE MONSTER: He said they are.

ME: I don't want to be crazy.

LITTLE MONSTER: You are. You have to fix it.

ME: You're right. I have to go back.

LITTLE MONSTER: Wait. I was wrong. Don't you dare turn this car around.

ME: You just told me to go back!

LITTLE MONSTER: Wait, yeah go back!

ME: I'm so confused.

LITTLE MONSTER: He might decide he hates you overnight. Go back and make sure that doesn't happen. But also don't go back because he might think you're crazy if you go back.

ME: WHAT!?

LITTLE MONSTER: The stakes are so high!! He thinks you're crazy!

ME: He's right.

LITTLE MONSTER: You need to prove to him that you're not crazy.

NARRATOR: I pulled my car over, and sat shaking by the side of the road. And then, I turned around. And drove back to Chad's house. I knocked on the door and ... surprise! He was still there! But he was not happy with me. That was the slippery moment when I started ruining everything.

***

NARRATOR: Okay time for a check in! Not so bad yet. This last bit was kinda my fault, right? Like, the way he was acting changed and his boundaries changed kinda quickly, and he called me "crazy" which we all know isn't cool, but it's also nothing to cause a scene about ... and I also freaked out! Like, I was a LOT.

Right?

Was I?

Let's keep going, shall we?

KATI SCHWARTZ

BAD PEOPLE

PART II - The Part That Started Around The Time I Tried To Face The Horizon, Stretch My Arms Out, And Say , "I Accept And Love Myself Exactly As I Am." And I Then Thought, "That's Not Possible."

THE TRIGGERED

NARRATOR: For the first six months or so after my loss, every moment felt like:

ME: I miss them I miss them I miss them I miss them I miss them I miss them I miss them I miss them ....

NARRATOR: Thanks to hard work and the healing power of time, most days aren't as painful as that anymore. However, I have become a TRIGGER MONSTER. The weirdest, most mundane, unlikely things can still transform me from a functioning human being into a twitchy, writhing mess. The truth is, when you lose something or someone you love, it leaves a hole in you the exact size of what you lost, and it's so easy to let your surroundings remind you of that. Some of my favorite triggers include: children, good coffee (bad coffee is okay), airports, my phone, Sharpies, comfortable couches (uncomfortable ones are okay), sand, socks, food delivery, bean bags, open flame, and literally any animal. Now, having joined the ranks of "The Triggered," as I like to call us, I have such compassion for anyone who has felt surrounded and suffocated by constant reminders of their distress. To everyone I rolled my eyes at: you are right - no one's pain should be mocked or minimized by anyone else. That said, in the spirit of finding humor within my personal tragedies, I would like to share with you some of my more ridiculous triggers:

SUNSHINE

While everyone's enjoying the beautiful weather, I've been known to hide under my tiny personal rain cloud, spiralling into allthegoodtimesIhadinthesunshinebeforeIruinedmylifeandlost everythingthisremindsmeofthattimewesatonthelawninthesunor thetimewewenthikingorthetimewesaidthesunisinmyeyesohmy godpleasejustrain.

SUSHI

Pro tip: if you're triggered by sushi, avoid the pre-packed meal section of Trader Joe's.

PASSENGER SEAT OF MY CAR

It's easy to glance over to my right when driving and remember the people who used to sit there.

FEBREEZE

No excuses for this one.

MUSIC

I still live in fear that one of Chad's songs will come on the radio. It's happened a few times and I've turned into a flailing screaming maniac. For a while, my solution was to cut music out of my life altogether.

The first song that broke my 8 month silent streak was "These Dreams" by Heart. Speaking of which...

BAD PEOPLE

BAD PEOPLE

KATI SCHWARTZ

BAD PEOPLE

KATI SCHWARTZ

THE DAY THE MUSIC DIED

ALEX: What kind of music do you like?

NARRATOR: This is Alex. She and I met working together for a merchandise company that sells t-shirts at Broadway shows.

ALEX: People who don't like music are psychopaths.

NARRATOR: I met Michael at work, too. Same job.

MICHAEL: I brought you a cookie!

NARRATOR: This is Logan. Alex introduced me to him. Sometimes I think she wishes she hadn't because ....

LOGAN: (Screaming.) YOU CAN'T ORDER THE ONE RING ON ETSY AND WEAR IT TO COMICON BECAUSE IF YOU PUT IT ON YOU'LL DISAPPEAR AND SAURON WILL KNOW WHERE YOU ARE!!!

ME: YES!!! YOU GET IT!!!

LOGAN: WHY DOES EVERYONE THINK THIS IS OKAY!?!?

ME: I'VE BEEN ASKING MYSELF THAT QUESTION FOR YEARS!!!

NARRATOR: ... we're a lot. Although they knew nothing of what I'd been though, they were my first friends since LA.

One day in my first winter back in New York, I accompanied Alex to a record store in the east village. It was the first time since leaving LA that I'd willingly entered a place where music would be playing. And when I say willingly, I mean Alex kinda ... dragged me in there. Because the thing is, at that time I associated music entirely with being in LA and with Chad. Alex and I entered the record store, and music was not only playing, but celebrated. Band posters were plastered on every wall. There was nowhere I could look where I wasn't being bombarded with the very existence of music.

So we were in this music riddled record store, and Alex asked me what kind of music I liked. Hearing that question from her, someone I'd gotten to know closely over the past few months, felt akin to being asked what color your eyes are by someone who's staring right at you. For as long as I could remember, my specific music taste had been one of the biggest parts of my identity. I didn't know how to answer her.

ME: I used to like Jefferson Airplane, I guess.

ALEX: Yeah but what about now?

ME: I guess I like that song that Justin Bieber sings in Spanish.

ALEX: ...

ME: I like it because I can't really understand it.

ALEX: ...

ME: So it doesn't remind me of anything bad.

ALEX: I thought you spoke Spanish.

ME: Yeah but I'm not as good at it as I am at English.

ALEX: ... So you like top 40s music?

ME: I don't know. Not really.

NARRATOR: The truth was, I hadn't listened to music in eight months. Each song I had ever known and loved had become entwined in the painful experiences and losses of the past year. As a means of avoiding the crushing grief that music brought on, I filled my ears only with *Lord of The Rings* audio books, and avoided any public place that might be playing music. Coffee shops and clothing stores were avoided at all costs, and my phone was always out of data from playing Netflix through my headphones while I walked. Until my afternoon in the record shop with Alex, it had seemed like an acceptable solution. Now, watching her rifle through boxes of dusty records, I saw that my new music free existence couldn't be the solution to my sadness. I couldn't hide from music forever. There's a weird ass Jefferson Starship album called Blows Against The Empire that my dad taught me to love. The B side of the album chronicles a group of hippies who hijack a space craft, flee the planet Earth, and create a commune in outer space. I played it for my friend Gemma once but she didn't really "get it" and I didn't really "appreciate that," so I didn't play it for anyone else. Until I met Chad.

    Setting: Chad's gross living room couch, which Ellen calls "the sex couch." He and I are both on the sex couch, heads on opposite ends, feet meeting in the middle. We're just finishing a 17 minute song by Genesis.

ME: That was a great song.

CHAD: Yeah. Sometimes I listen to that song and imagine a wizard running through a field.

NARRATOR: He got me.

CHAD: Music is such a big part of me. It's like ... my soul.

ME: I feel the same way.

CHAD: You have good taste in music. For a girl.

NARRATOR: I was so flattered.

ME: Thank you.

CHAD: I didn't know girls could like rock and roll.

NARRATOR: I was so flattered.

ME: All my friends in high school just liked top 40s shit. But I was already listening to like, The Grateful Dead and stuff like that.

CHAD: You're not like other girls.

ME: Can I play you Blows Against The Empire?

CHAD: I don't have the energy to talk to you anymore, but I can do 45 minutes of music.

NARRATOR: For the next 45 minutes, he shushed me when I spoke over the song, contradicting himself only to murmur words like:

CHAD: Outstanding.

NARRATOR: Or:

CHAD: Beautiful.

NARRATOR: He grunted happily as Grace Slick crooned "you're old and your hands are gray." He bobbed his head from side to side. At the end, he said:

CHAD: Wild.

NARRATOR: He got it.

When I lost contact with Chad, music became an immediate and intense trigger no matter the situation. It got to the point where someone could twang a single note on a banjo string and I'd start flailing. One time, I was at a routine chiropractor appointment, and Dr. Kerr had just coerced my neck into alignment. I was alone in the room, having been ordered to lie still for a few minutes and let the adjustment set, when "Big Wheel" by Rush came onto the radio. It was one of Chad's favorites, and one he and I had oft listened to while having deep talks about life. I crammed my fingers into my ears in an attempt to block out the song and the painful memories it would surely evoke, but I could still hear the electric guitar solo pounding inside my head. So I began rapidly moving my fingers in and out of my ears, creating a noisy suction sound which helped somewhat, except for the millisecond when my fingers were fully removed and tiny bursts of song could sneak in. To combat that, I started rhythmically banging my heels against the table, and just for good measure moved my head from side to side so my hair would brush against the pillow and make a blanket of white noise.

DR. KERR: What's going on?

NARRATOR: This is Dr. Kerr.

DR. KERR: Are you having a seizure?

ME: A little.

NARRATOR: He had to realign my neck again as I had not held still as directed.

Coworkers became reluctantly used to my desperate bellows to change the song. Friends understood that if I showed up to a coffee date with a limp, it was likely that a troublesome song had come on in the grocery store and I'd twisted my ankle fleeing. Strangers on the subway withdrew in fear as I berated young men for playing ACDC aloud from their phones, accusing them of "subjecting me to emotional distress during my commute." Another time, this happened:

Setting: Me and a woman on a maybe date in a place that isn't sure if it's a café or a 70's bar. It's Christmas and I'm fighting to combat that I'm single on a holiday feeling.

ME: I think music is a disrespectful and unnecessary part of our culture.

COFFEE MEETS BAGEL GIRL: ... what culture?

ME: Our culture.

CMBG: I saw a Robyn concert last week.

ME: I'm more into nature sounds right now.

CMBG: I'm gonna go.

NARRATOR: That spring, Alex was sent on a work trip to Durham, North Carolina. Itching for some travel, I tagged along. We were in our rental Subaru Legacy when These Dreams by Heart came on the radio. Immediately, I was accosted by a memory of listening to the same song while picking up Chad from LAX. I felt myself begin the descent into my all too familiar spiral.

ALEX: Oh my god this song is a JAMMER!!!

ME: I don't like this song.

ALEX: (Singing.) THE SWEETEST SONG IS SILENCE THAT I'VE EVER HEARD!!

ME: Can we turn the music off?

ALEX: Why? I love this song!

ME: It's just ....

ALEX: (Singing.) FUNNY HOW YOUR FEET IN DREAMS NEVER TOUCH THE EARTH

ME: It makes me think of ....

ALEX: (Singing.) IN A WOOD FULL OF PRINCES ....

ME: This is triggering.

NARRATOR: But then, my little monster and I had a different sort of talk :

ME: Are you really going to let some asshole take your music?

LITTLE MONSTER: Yeah. It's safer.

ME: No you're not.

NARRATOR: The more I attempted to protest, the louder Alex's singing grew.

ALEX: (Singing.) THESE DREAMS GO ON WHEN I CLOSE MY EYES. EVERY SECOND OF THE NIGHT I LIVE ANOTHER LIFE!!

NARRATOR: By the final notes, the song belonged to me. All other memories of that song ... any hold Chad had on it ... it was replaced by Alex.

[A robotic voice says "POWER UP! You've earned the power to reclaim your music!" like in Scott Pilgrim vs. the world.]

NARRATOR (CONT'D): I stole that from Scott Pilgrim vs. The World.

ME: The music came back to me on it's own, when it was ready. And maybe they will, too?

***

NARRATOR: Hi everyone! Just checking in. I know ... that last part was so sweet. That story with Alex? Such a cute one.

Picture this next part as a gigantic middle finger.

KATI SCHWARTZ

BAD PEOPLE

PART III — There Are Some Things That I'm Finally Ready To Say Like They Are And Not Make Them Seem Better Or Different Than They Were.

BAD PEOPLE

THE JOURNAL

NARRATOR: So at this point in my weird journey, my little monster was basically always sitting on my shoulder and repeatedly screaming two things into my ear. The first one was:

LITTLE MONSTER: DON'T. TRUST. ANYONE. THEY WILL ABANDON YOU.

NARRATOR: The second one was:

LITTLE MONSTER: DON'T. TELL. ANYONE. ANYTHING. IT WILL MAKE THEM HATE YOU.

NARRATOR: This crazed, screaming little monster created unfortunate situations:

   Setting: 1 Train platform. Logan is getting on the train.

LOGAN: See you later.

NARRATOR: Logan steps into the train car. In one impressive motion, I grab his shirt and pull him off of the train. The doors close. We fall backwards onto the platform, me sobbing into his shirt.

ME: Don't leave me!

LOGAN: ... I'm just going to Trader Joe's.

NARRATOR: Or this:

   Setting: Bar. Michael and I are having a drink after work. I'm sweating profusely and my hands were balled into fists.

MICHAEL: What's up?

ME: Nothing.

MICHAEL: Well, I brought you a cookie because it looks like you're having a bad -

ME: I'VE NEVER BEEN BETTER!!!

NARRATOR: Sweating through hangouts with new friends isn't fun or sustainable, so I decided to see a therapist who could help me not be such a mess. She taught me some tools to quiet my little monster. These tools included listing three things I'm grateful for each morning, and going for runs as a form of "active meditation." She also suggested I keep a journal documenting my use of said tools and noting the results:

ME: (Reading aloud from journal.)

6/10/19

Dear Journal,

I've started a gratitude practice. Every evening, I take time to focus on what I'm grateful for. But no matter how much I try to force my thoughts to my friends and family, I just feel unending gratitude for my Nintendo Switch. It brings me intense joy in the way no living thing could. I feel bad about that but it's my truth. Those three Amazon gift cards were spent wisely.

6/30/18

Dear Journal,

My little monster was ruining my day today, so I decided to go for a run. I put on those free leggings and my shirt that says, "You are filled with determination" because I guess I am, and a bandana with tacos on it. I was also wearing those orange running shoes from Goodwill that are two sizes too big. I always trip when I wear them because they're huge, so I focused on picking up my feet, but then I switched to focusing on meditating while I run. As soon as I did that, though, my big ass shoes hit a tree root and I went flying. It's super hot and hasn't rained in a while so the ground is all dust, so when I hit the ground it was more of a ploof than a crash. I got up right away and kept running because doing so felt like a metaphor for my life, but then I quickly noticed that people were looking at me strangely. One woman actually crossed to the other side of the running path. I thought maybe they were intimidated by my no nonsense "when you knock me down I get the fuck back up again" attitude, until I got back home and looked in the mirror. I guess when I ploofed, all the dust on the ground went up in the air and then stuck to my sweaty head. I looked like I'd covered myself in orange self-tanner. My sweat had then created rivulets through the dust so it looked like I had gross sweat riverbeds all over my face. My free leggings were ripped and my knee was bleeding. Some of the blood from the wound must have gotten on my hand, because a red, murdery splotch of it was smeared across my forehead. To top it off, the bandana had come loose and was flapping above my head like some sort of weird tropical bird feathers. I looked so dumb.

7/18/19

I decided to tell Alex what I went through in LA because apparently it's important that I do so. I guess keeping everything a secret just makes it all bigger. I was about to tell her, but then my little monster chimed in and shut it down. So instead I told her the story of when a chihuahua chased me on a razor scooter. I think she was super confused because I built it up like I was going to tell her something big. I'm too scared though. I don't even know if it's a trust thing or just a matter of saying the things out loud at all. I'm too scared to tell her about therapy. She sent me a text once saying that I was "well adjusted," and if she knows I go to therapy she might not think that anymore. I'm too scared to tell her that I'm realizing that I'm not entirely at fault in the loss of my friends. I alluded to her so many times that I did something bad that drove everyone away. Explaining that the situation is so, so much more complicated than that, that I was driven to dire straights because Chad was abandoning me. The thought that those people were perhaps unkind, is terrifying and unimaginable. I'm too scared to tell her about situations like:

Setting: Los Angeles Comicon. December. A deserted hallway at a convention center. I'm talking to Marcy, my current girlfriend.

MARCY: Chad signed his name on his wrist and then I tattooed it there.

ME: Whoa. That's ... cool I guess.

MARCY: He has all his fans do that.

ME: Or this:

NARRATOR: Setting: Sidewalk. It's nighttime.

ME: You cheated on me with Chad?

MARCY: I'm so sorry. He made me.

ME: Or this one:

NARRATOR: Setting: My apartment in Glendale.

MARCY: I want to be in an open relationship.

ME: I want to be monogamous.

MARCY: You'd still be my primary. It's just I'm in love with Chad, and he told me he loved me, too. But I also love you!

ME: You can't date Chad and also be my girlfriend.

ME: Or this one:

NARRATOR: Setting: FaceTime.

MARCY: I had a threesome with Chad.

ME: Again?

MARCY: Just listen for a second.

ME: I don't know what to say. I forgave you for cheating on me with him once, but ….

MARCY: Listen. It was horrible. I think he's a ….

ME: Don't make excuses.

ME (CONT'D): I'm too scared to tell her about the things he did to Marcy. That he messages girls twenty years younger than him and then uses them for sex. I'm too scared to tell her that I didn't listen to Marcy, and that for the first time in my life I understand women who don't come forward in the Me Too movement. I'm too scared to say that I was paid $200 to change a powerful man's bed sheets so he could abuse his power with young women. That this man compared himself to the Dali Lama. That my therapist described him as a cult leader. I'm too scared to say that I found ways to justify his behavior because I needed him. I'm too scared to say that I still miss him. That I still send him birthday wishes even though I'm sure he blocked me from his phone. I miss him even though I'm horrified by him. If I tell people the truth I feel like I'll never see Chad again. I'm scared to say that I want to see him again. Do other people feel that way?

8/7/18

Dear Journal,

I'm babysitting for another hour. Both children are asleep, thank god. I made a note to myself in my planner to journal about my little monster, but I don't want to because I don't want to think about those things.

NARRATOR: That was my last journal entry. I decided that the tools were bullshit and more hurtful than helpful. The thing about therapists, at least the good ones, is that they're what Gollum would call "tricksy." They know more about the inner workings of the human brain than their patients do, and will lead you into moments of great healing often without you realizing that's what they're doing. Within about two weeks of writing my last journal entry, I found myself in the Following situation:

Setting: Couch. Messy apartment. Two people playing Super Mario Brothers on Nintendo Switch.

ALEX: Jump on my head! I'll launch you onto the platform and you can get the third big coin!

ME: Hey, before we do that, can I tell you something?

ALEX: Just get the coin first!

ME: You're not launching me correctly!

ALEX: Don't go into the bubble! I might fall off the mushroom and then we'll both be dead!

ME: Too late!!

ALEX: Damnit!

ME: Now that we're both dead, can I tell you something?

NARRATOR: She listened. I told her everything. We're still friends.

[The same robotic voice from before says "POWER UP! You've earned the power of radical honesty!"]

KATI SCHWARTZ

BAD PEOPLE

HEALTHY RELATIONSHIPS

NARRATOR: Unhealthy relationships are so fun. They're fun in the same way The Superman Roller Coaster at Six Flags that hellish ride once when I was fourteen. The series of events were exhausting.

1.) I wait in line with my friends for two hours.

2.) We ride to the top. We're admiring the sun-bleached tops of the various rides, but also laugh sobbing a little because we aren't sure if we're about to have an amazing time or die.

3.) We drop so far for so long at such a steep angle that we're practically upside down. I enter a primal fight for survival.

4.) After the first drop is over, the peaks and drops are so fun that my tummy flips in a fun tickly way.

5.) This repeats itself maybe 10 times through out the ride. It's a dramatic and constant shift between joy and misery. And good god it's exhausting, but I'm also sort of willing to wait another two hours in line to do it again (we didn't pay for those passes that let you skip the line).

The roller coaster-esque ups of unhealthy relationships are addictive. The downs are dramatic and so painful, but the ups are euphoric and make the downs feel worth enduring. When I first started forming healthy relationships, I was bored as shit. That's because, if I'm being honest with myself, not all of my conversations with Chad were about chodes (I'm in the honest section of this piece now). I was very used to this:

Going up.

Setting: Chad's house. Two hours ago, I was in Disney Land with a friend who was visiting from the east coast, but made up an excuse to leave because Chad asked if I could hang out. I dropped everything and drove 90 minutes from Anaheim to his house.

CHAD: We should have a "fourgy." We can find three women to have sex with us and pass them between us.

ME: Haha.

NARRATOR: Was he getting aroused?

CHAD: That would be so hot. If I ever have a fourgy I can retire from sex forever. It's my ultimate fantasy.

ME: Wouldn't it be a fivegy? You and me plus three women?

CHAD: Yeah but you and I wouldn't touch each other.

ME: Is that a Super Nintendo by your TV?

CHAD: I have such a crazy boner right now.

ME: That's ... okay.

CHAD: You're such a cool girl. I can't talk to just anyone about my ultimate fantasies.

NARRATOR: The peak.

Setting: On set for one of Chad's music videos. We're on a break. He's scratching my head and hugging me close.

ME: I love head scratches.

CHAD: I know you do.

[Beat.]

CHAD (CONT'D): Who needs to be paid when you get head scratches from your rockstar big brother?

NARRATOR: Going down.

Setting: A party.

RANDOM MALE FRIEND: Her?

CHAD: Yeah.

RANDOM MALE FRIEND: Hey.

ME: Hey.

RANDOM MALE FRIEND: Wanna lick my butthole?

NARRATOR: Chad laughs so hard.

CHAD: You can say anything to that girl!

NARRATOR: The down.

   Setting: Chad's recording studio. I'm there volunteering as a production assistant.

CHAD: If I give you fifty thousand dollars will you leave me alone?

ME: I'm sorry.

CHAD: You're a bad person.

ME: I'm a bad person.

NARRATOR: That's the first time I took on that label.

CHAD: Great. Thank you.

NARRATOR: After that, it was internalized.

   Going up.

   Ten minutes later.

ME: Can I talk to you for a second?

CHAD: Yup.

ME: I know I'm a piece of shit but you don't have to be an asshole about it.

NARRATOR: Chad puts his hand on my heart. He picks up my hand and puts it over his heart. We look into each other's eyes.

CHAD: Breathe with me.

NARRATOR: The peak.

Setting: The sex couch. Chad grabs my face and aggressively kisses my cheek.

CHAD: I love you!!!

NARRATOR: And this:

Going up.

Setting: Ellen's house. Ellen is SO COOL. I have a cat in my lap.

ELLEN: Wow, my cat really likes you. She doesn't like anyone.

NARRATOR: The peak.

    Setting: A theater.

ELLEN: Your play was amazing. I think you're one of the most incredible artists I've ever met.

ME: Oh my god. Thank you.

ELLEN: I draw but my art is shit.

ME: Don't say that.

ELLEN: I think you're a better writer than Chad.

ME: Whoa, really?

ELLEN: Yeah. I think his song lyrics are awful. But please don't tell anyone.

NARRATOR: The down.

    Setting: Ellen's house. Nighttime. She was trying to smash her head into the corner of a doorframe. She was screaming.

ELLEN: I hate myself!

ME: Stop!

NARRATOR: Ellen smashed her head. I tackled her to the ground. She remained in child's pose on the rug.

ELLEN: I'm trying not to hurt myself. Chad is going to have the group kick me out.

ME: Just keep screaming.

[She screams.]

ELLEN: Does blood wash out of fabric?

NARRATOR: I ran out of the house. I drove to Chad's place.

The peak.

A letter addressed to me from Ellen:

ELLEN: Holy shit girl, You saved my life. You are so good. I hope you know that, no matter what, you are good. Let's be best fairy friends forever, okay?

NARRATOR: The down.

Setting: Text message from Ellen.

ELLEN: I would never tell you to disappear.

ME: I am worse than those twelve year old girls.

NARRATOR: It was all actually really dangerous. Now, for the first time in my life, I have healthy friends and relationships. More often than not, healthy relationships look something like:

LOGAN: Wanna watch a movie?

ME: Sure!

NARRATOR: We watched a movie.

THAT'S THE END OF THE SCENE!!!!! DO YOU SEE WHY I WAS CONFUSED!!?!?!?!??!?!

It turns out, though, that healthy friendships have big ups, too.

Setting: My crappy New York apartment.

ME: Thanks for coming over for Hanukkah you guys!

ALEX: I brought face paint!

EVERYONE: Sweeeeet!

LOGAN: Make my face green! I love green!

ME: Can someone write "Fly you fools!" on my forehead!?

MICHAEL: Face paint is great for your pores.

NARRATOR: There's nothing dangerous about face paint. (It even washes out of fabrics.)

BAD PEOPLE

MIDDLE EARTH

NARRATOR: I recently made the casual decision to just get over all of this and be all better.

[The robotic voice says "POWER U - wait never mind."]

NARRATOR (CONT'D): My little monster started it.

LITTLE MONSTER: Why are you choosing to still let that stuff bother you?

ME: I can't help it.

LITTLE MONSTER: Get over it!!

ME: I think I need time to heal and process.

LITTLE MONSTER: You're CHOOSING to still be upset. Just CHOOSE to be happy! It's that easy!

NARRATOR: I listened to my little monster, and told my therapist about my little "choose happy" epiphany. She was less than impressed. The thing is, I have a tendency to be incredibly stubborn and unflinching. And the thing about that is ... while sometimes stubbornness can keep you safe, sometimes it can keep you in a dangerous situations.

Looking back on my time with Chad, there are literally hundreds and hundreds of red flags that I stubbornly ignored. For example:

Setting: FaceTime with a friend from home. This was months before I was kicked out.

ME: Things are getting a little better. I have still been breaking a lot of rules, but -

FRIEND: Rules? Whose rules?

ME: - but luckily Chad has been merciful.

FRIEND: Merciful?

ME: He's going to pay for me to go to a self help retreat so that I'll stop being so difficult for him to be around.

FRIEND: That sounds ... weird.

ME: What!? It's so nice of him. It's $5000 so I could never go on my own.

FRIEND: FIVE THOUSAND DOLLARS!?

ME: He sent a few other people there, too. He said it'll keep our relationship alive. I'm just too much right now.

FRIEND: What is this self help retreat? And why does he have so much money?

ME: It's called the Steiner Institute.

FRIEND: That sounds like a cult.

ME: He said it's going to make me better. So I'm going.

NARRATOR: Cut to after I was kicked out:

ME: The Institute worked for everyone else Chad sent there. Why didn't it work for me?

LITTLE MONSTER: Who knows. I guess you're not fixable.

ME: I'm starting to think Chad wasn't very nice.

LITTLE MONSTER: Who cares? Don't think about it. You're over it.

NARRATOR: To prove to myself how over it I was, I recently met up with Diane.

I first met Diane in LA through Chad. Although she and Chad were very close and often slept together, she was always on the outskirts of the "friend group." Seeing her that day, I'd decided that there was no way I was going to bring up Chad with her.

Setting: New York City coffee shop.

ME: So how's Chad?

DIANE: I don't really know. I don't hear from him as much as I used to.

ME: Really? But you two were so close.

DIANE: I messed things up. I caught feelings and asked if we could be monogamous. He told me I was being clingy.

ME: Oh my god.

DIANE: I told him I could be okay with him sleeping with other women as long as they were in other cities. I don't see why he would need to sleep with so many people in Los Angeles. He said okay, but then he slept with more people in LA without telling me.

ME: Oh my god.

DIANE: There was one morning I slept with him and then I'm pretty sure he changed his sheets and slept with someone else that night. Who knows maybe he changed the sheets twice and slept with three girls that day.

NARRATOR: I changed those sheets. He paid me $200 to do it. Remember when I said I could ignore red flags?

DIANE: It's okay. It's just who he is. I still love him.

ME: You do?

DIANE: Oh yeah. Sometimes he sends me a meme and it makes my day. I basically sit around all day looking at my phone hoping that he'll send me a meme.

ME: How often does he send you a meme?

DIANE: Like, once every two weeks.

NARRATOR: I knew from my time spent with him that every once in a while he would send a meme out to all the women he was sleeping with. It was to make them feel special. But the reality was, he sent the same meme to all those women at once.

DIANE: I'd rather share him with a lot of other women than not have him at all.

ME: ...

DIANE: At least I didn't get dumped like a lot of the girls who got too clingy.

ME: Dumped?

DIANE: He dumps everyone. Everyone in that group of friends does. They dump anyone who does anything wrong.

ME: They dumped me.

DIANE: Actually, Ellen just got dumped.

ME: She did?

DIANE: They have such a weird way of handling things.

ME: I guess ... I kinda knew that from the start. Sort of. I just never thought it could happen to me.

DIANE: They thrive on dumping people.

ME: You don't find that horrible?

DIANE: I do. But what are you going to do about it?

ME: Stop sleeping with Chad?

DIANE: No I don't want to do that. What we have now is healthy.

ME: ...

DIANE: If it wasn't, he would have gotten rid of me already like he does with most of his girls.

NARRATOR: His girls. HIS girls. That was the start of me realizing that I was one body in a graveyard of Chad's used and discarded people. Hearing Diane say that, I decided to look him up on Google - something I'd never done before. I'll never forget what I found:

[The disembodied voices of Chad's victims float in. Maybe they overlap.]

VOICE 1: I met him at his concert.

VOICE 2: I was such a big fan of his music.

VOICE 3: I'd just turned eighteen.

VOICE 4: He gave me what I needed. He saw me and then he used me.

VOICE 5: What was I to him? Something warm?

VOICE 6: Chad asked me to build an empire with him. Those were his exact words.

VOICE 7: He told me he loved me.

VOICE 8: He told me I wasn't like other girls.

VOICE 9: When I fell in love back, he threw me out.

VOICE 10: He taught me to trust him first.

VOICE 11: He told me I was family.

VOICE 12: He only used me for threesomes.

VOICE 13: When I said I wouldn't sleep with him, he asked me to feel his erection.

VOICE 14: He asked for naked pictures and then called me crazy.

VOICE 15: Sharon and I were best friends. When I wouldn't have a threesome with Chad, he told her not to speak to me again. She listened.

VOICE 16: I was 18. He was 39.

VOICE 17: I was 20. He was in his late thirties.

VOICE 18: When he found out I was 30, he said I was too old for him. He was forty.

VOICE 19: He offered me money to leave him alone.

VOICE 20: He's the leader of that group. They do whatever he says.

VOICE 21: I can't help but feel such shame about it. Who was that man?

VOICE 22: He says I made the whole thing up. That I'm lying for attention.

[The voices float away.]

NARRATOR: His pattern of abuse was suddenly glaringly clear. He'd done the same thing to all these young women. To me. He'd:

Found us.

Brought us in.

Used us.

Spit us out.

[Beat.]

ME: I'm jealous of you.

DIANE: Jealous?

ME: Why is he in touch with you and not me?

NARRATOR: I was his garbage. Why did I miss him?

DIANE: Well, did you ever apologize for what you did?

NARRATOR: The document was readily available in my pocket. I read it to her:

ME: (Reading aloud.) My beloved friends,

I feel it's time to ask for your forgiveness as a community. If I can forgive myself, I know you can forgive me, too. The simple explanation of what happened is that I acted like my worst self because Chad was pulling away. I think all of us have an idea that emotional pain can be easily set aside with enough mind power. That mindset did me a disservice. I tried to use quick fixes to solve enormous problems and didn't realize how intense my abandonment issues were until I told that lie to Sharon. It's hard to speak the love I have for all of you, and the amount of regret I have for how I hurt you (although the person who I hurt more than anyone is myself). Please know that even in the height of this crisis that I caused, not one day passed when I didn't feel authentic love and gratitude for all of you. You were never taken for granted. Your love taught me what it means to really connect with another person, and what true friendship is. I know that am going to make many, many more mistakes in my life, but I will never again make the same ones that hurt all of you. That's a promise. We have all done things out of character that have scared other people and ourselves. I am so proud of the work I've done to fix myself.

NARRATOR: Fix myself.

ME: I don't expect to be welcomed back in the same way I was before - I'm expecting some understandable trepidation from all of you. I am moving back to LA next week, though, and I truly hope you give me the chance to slowly reintegrate with your beautiful community in a way that is much healthier for everyone than it was before.

Humbly,

Me.

NARRATOR: I'd sent that three months after they cut me out.

DIANE: You didn't move back to LA though.

ME: They never responded.

DIANE: Oh.

ME: Not one of them. So I didn't go back.

DIANE: All because of that text to Ellen?

ME: Yeah.

DIANE: But it was so … forgivable.

ME: I guess Chad used it as an excuse to get rid of me.

DIANE: Oh well. That's just what Chad does when he's done with people. He loves being in charge of who his friends hate. Don't take it personally! Will it upset you if I show you the meme Chad sent me this morning? It's really funny.

***

NARRATOR: Here's how I wish my conversation with Diane went.

DIANE: It's okay, It's just who he is. I still love him.

ME: That's ... disgusting.

DIANE: Me?

ME: Not you. Him. He's Awful.

DIANE: But I love him. You just don't get it.

ME: He doesn't love you. He never did. He never loved any of us. We're just ... toys to him. And you don't deserve that. None of us do. I deserve better. I ... Fuck him. Fuck all those people who follow him. He's not who he says he is. He's not the Dali Lama. He's a fake. A dangerous fake. He's ... they're like a cult. They follow him just because he's a charismatic, powerful man with long hair! None of them ever cared about me. And I gave them myself. I gave them me but they only wanted him. I didn't do anything wrong. I told a lie about Ellen. I made a mistake. I made ... I deserve Alex. I deserve Logan. Real friends who love me. We deserve love, Diane! We deserve more than Chad.

DIANE: ... Holy shit. You're right.

NARRATOR: That would have been better.

* * *

NARRATOR: Okay, let's stop for a second. Just, stop everything for a moment because the show is almost over, and I just want to make sure no one is confused. Because ... this is currently my thirteenth draft of this show ... after draft number twelve, I had to revise again, because there was some confusion

... an old friend of mine saw it, and we had an interaction that went something like this:

Setting: And old friend and I are talking on the phone. I'm in New York, and he's somewhere else. He just saw a video of my show.

OLD FRIEND: So, what do you want?

ME: Huh?

OLD FRIEND: Why did you write this play? What did you want to happen?

ME: Uh ....

OLD FRIEND: I just don't understand what you want. Do you want to ruin his life?

NARRATOR: Let's set something straight: this will never be the right thing to say to someone.

OLD FRIEND: Wouldn't you feel better if you just let it go?

NARRATOR: To avoid future misinterpretations like this one, I've decided to take a moment to be explicit. Here's what I (and draft thirteen) want you to understand: This is not a personal vendetta against someone who wronged me. This is not an attempt to "ruin anyone's life." This is not me begging or pleading for anything. That's what the first six or seven drafts were. This is me DEMANDING you to stop defending dangerous men. That's what this whole thing is about. This ...

OLD FRIEND: I don't understand ... do you want to ruin his life?

NARRATOR: ... is defending a dangerous man. This ....

AUNT'S FACEBOOK STATUS: Why can't everyone just leave Louis C. K. alone?

NARRATOR: ...is defending a dangerous man. This ....

BARISTA 1: I'm telling the boss that Nate showed me a photo of his dick at work.

BARISTA 2: Please don't do that. He's just sad because his dad has cancer.

NARRATOR: ... I shouldn't have to explain, but ... THIS IS DEFENDING A DANGEROUS MAN!!! Those are all REAL LIFE examples!! Can someone bring me a soapbox please!?

STOP DEFENDING DANGEROUS MEN!!! STOP DOING IT!! I DON'T CARE HOW FUNNY THEY ARE! I DON'T CARE IF THEY ARE SAD!! I DON'T CARE IF THEY REGRET THEIR OWN SHITTY BEHAVIOR!! STOP!!! DEFENDING!!! THEM!!!

NARRATOR (CONT'D): That's all. Now, let's finish up the show.

* * *

NARRATOR: I went home and played this really depressing video game on my Nintendo Switch called Gris. In the start of the game, the character you're playing as is so grief laden that she falls to her knees each time you press A to make her jump. It looked satisfying, so I tried to do it in real life, but doing so really hurt my knees and made such a loud crash on the floor that my downstairs neighbor started pounding on her ceiling with a broom handle. As I listened to her crashing around below me, praying that she wouldn't call the superintendent, my phone chimed. It was Logan. It said:

LOGAN: Hey! Wanna watch a movie?

NARRATOR: He came over. He listened and understood. He wasn't driven away. And then we watched the movie. And that was the end of the scene.

[The robotic voice says "POWER UP! You've earned the power of resilience!"]

NARRATOR (CONT'D): The movie we watched, if you can believe it, was *Lord of The Rings*. The *Fellowship of the Ring*, to be precise.

LOGAN: (Imitating Bilbo Baggins.) I feel thin, sort of stretched, like butter scraped over too much bread.

ME: You get me.

NARRATOR: Watching it, I was struck by the similarity between Chad and The One Ring. Being connected to someone like Chad is like being the ring bearer. The thing you possess is sickeningly seductive. It's powerful enough to make you overlook anything. You're chosen. I was chosen. I was loved by someone who was selective beyond measure. And he selected me. Everyone else in the group followed suit.

Losing a friendship like that is like losing the ring. You go to all ends to get it back. You feel like you'll die without it. But once it's gone, it's gone. And I'm realizing ... maybe that's a good thing.

Now that Chad's out of my life, it's my job to own up to the role I played in his mistreatment of women. To apologize, and begin the ongoing process of forgiving myself for it. Watching the movie with a good friend by my side, it's possible for just one moment to transport my self into Middle Earth. In this moment, I am the ring bearer. The friend next to me is my Samwise Gamgee. The ring is heavy and the string it hangs from leaves deep cuts on my neck. But I'm determined to make it through the gates of Mordor. I'm determined to destroy it. I've been trekking through the Misty Mountains for days. I've slept on the ground beneath trees and on top of rocks. I've only had lembas bread to eat and mucky water to drink since my journey started. At times, I've felt like giving up. I've wondered why this burden was given to me. But then I hear Gandalf's voice:

ME: (In the voice of Gandalf.) So do all who live to see such times. But that is not for you to decide. All we have to decide is what to do with the time that is given us.

NARRATOR: At that, I'm able to stand back up and look at the view. I'm higher up than I realized. In that fleeting moment, in the middle of my journey, for the first time I'm able to extend my arms to the mountains and the trees of Middle Earth and say "I accept and love myself exactly as I am." And for that one brief second, I'm able to believe it.

[End of Show.]

[Then ...]

Just to clarify: When I say I'm the ring bearer, I do NOT mean that I'm Frodo. He's useless. The first time he sees a Ringwraith, he drops his sword, falls over, and takes out the ring. I'd never do that. I'd stay on my feet and fight those bastards.

[Actual end of show.]

KATI SCHWARTZ

BAD PEOPLE

Made in the USA
Columbia, SC
01 December 2024